GRIZZLY
THE SPIRIT BEAR

WILLIAM HARLEY BROOKS

Copyright © 1999
William Harley Brooks

All rights reserved. No part of this book may be reproduced in any form, except for the inclusion of brief quotations in a review, without permission in writing from the author or publisher.

ISBN: 0-7392-0142-5

Library of Congress Catalog Card Number: 99-94823

Printed in the USA by

MORRIS PUBLISHING

3212 East Highway 30 • Kearney, NE 68847 • 1-800-650-7888

GRIZZLY, THE SPIRIT BEAR

TABLE OF CONTENTS

CHAPTER	PAGE
TABLE OF CONTENTS...............	I
DEDICATION..............................	iii
ABOUT THE AUTHOR...............	v
INTRODUCTION........................	vii
1. BEFORE THE PILGRIMS........	1
2. ONE EYE THE SNAKE BEAR..	5
3. CROSSING THE GREAT RIVER.....	35
4. THE MOUNTAIN MEN............	38
5. THE BUFFALO HUNTERS......	42
6. THE IMMIGRANTS.................	45
7. THE SETTLERS AND RANCHERS......	48
8. THE BOUNTY HUNTERS........	51
9. THE RAILROAD, TOWNS, & CITIES...	53
10. SPORT HUNTERS..................	57
11. HUNTERS IN GENERAL.......	60
12. THE LAST STAND.................	66
PHOTO GALLERY......................	70
ACKNOWLEDGMENTS..............	80

GRIZZLY, THE SPIRIT BEAR

ORDERING COPIES OF THIS BOOK........ 84

GRIZZLY, THE SPIRIT BEAR

DEDICATION

This book is dedicated to the memory of *Kanga*, the Author's beloved companion for many years. They were constant companions and stayed in the mountains whenever they could.

Kanga knew the Grizzlies and would run them off if they happen to have ventured into camp. They didn't like her

GRIZZLY, THE SPIRIT BEAR

barking and nipping. She was lucky to have survived those encounters with such a well-armed foe as a Grizzly. The only thing she ever feared was a flyswatter used for training.

There is a movie out I believe which is called "ALL DOGS GO TO HEAVEN." I know *Kanga* was here for me then and is there now waiting for me.

Thanks Kanga,

The Griz

GRIZZLY, THE SPIRIT BEAR

ABOUT THE AUTHOR

The author with a high mountain buck taken in a fair chase with a primitive weapon during the 1994 season. Now, the weapon of choice for the author is a camera. When good hunters reach their golden years, they seem to lose the desire to harvest animals. Instead, they become more interested in preserving what is left for others.

GRIZZLY, THE SPIRIT BEAR

This doesn't mean the author is against regulated hunting by others. Only, that he just doesn't want to take a life anymore. It is much too precious to him.

This deer was taken in heavy grizzly country where the author spent many years hunting and hiking. Often, he was within a stone's throw of many different Grizzlies and has yet to receive his first scratch from one of them. His rule is, if a grizzly found his kill before he got it out of the woods, then it belonged to the Bear.

The author has spent many happy days hiking inside the Yellowstone National Park and watching the Grizzlies. Such a place is soothing to me after my years in Viet Nam. Let us fight to keep such places pristine, managing wisely all of the creatures that belong there.

Sincerely the Author,

William Harley "The Griz" Brooks
M.S.C., U.S. Navy, Retired

GRIZZLY, THE SPIRIT BEAR

INTRODUCTION

This book will be done in a narrative form since we weren't there to see all that is depicted, but only those parts that we have experienced as an end result, and surely know.

Let's start with day one, or maybe I should say day six of the creation. We can't have it both ways. Either we are created beings produced by a superior being, or we are merely developed by chance in some stagnant swamp.

I have looked at this for many years and have read extensively on the subject which has brought me to the conclusion that life was produced by a higher being. That is, that most forms of life are connected to other forms of life. In other words, one can't exist without the other. What we call Spirit is hard to define, yet it can be determined, experienced, and is known to exist.

We humans are not the only ones who have a Spirit or inner being. All creatures have this feature.

Our Spirit Bear was wrongly named, the Horrible Bear. He is far from this term and mostly just wants a private life style within his range. We have driven him from the Great Plains into the Rocky Mountains where he is trying to make a last stand. Against modern weapons and human greed, this magnificent Bear has no chance to survive.

We, as humans, were appointed by a higher being as having dominion over all creatures. You cannot dominate over something that does not exist. We should know this after thousands of creatures that are no longer here because of our

GRIZZLY, THE SPIRIT BEAR

actions. Greed, stupidity, and ignorance are the driving forces that make us completely wipe out another species, with maybe a little fear thrown in.

Finally, some humans are waking up or wising up to what is happening. Perhaps we will be able to convince enough others that we need this Bear, and all other creatures that we have placed in dire circumstances.

Mother nature is all around us and is a very strong Spirit if we give her a chance. Our Grizzly has this strong Spirit and only needs a little room in what is left of our wilderness.

The North American continent with all of its great resources has made us the strongest nation in the world. Out of respect for the fragile balance in nature, we should set aside some of it to be wild forever.

This means helping those life forms in trouble and not weakening the laws that are in place to make this happen. A forest or plain without life forms is a very lonely and barren place in deed.

This book will be looking at things from the Grizzly's point of view and how he must have felt about our actions.

GRIZZLY, THE SPIRIT BEAR

GRIZZLY, THE SPIRIT BEAR

CHAPTER ONE:
BEFORE THE PILGRIMS

We the Bears, and "the people," kind of had an understanding and respect for each other. Fights did break out, but not often. We were kind of matched up. The people had spears, lances, and bows. We had our six inch claws, three inch fangs, and great strength.

The people were very wise in their movements and knew the terrain extremely well. Only rarely did they come to close to our sows with cubs. In turn, when that event occurred, the sows would feel the need to charge. Many times it was only a bluff intended to frighten, but when the real thing went down, the fight would be vicious, ending with many wounds and sometimes death. Often, our sows would die of those terrible lance wounds and the thrust of spears, but you can be assured that the people would pay a high price from our claws and fangs.

Sometimes a fight would break out over food when we were hungry and we had brought a kill down. I guess we felt we were the rulers of the plains and mountains, and in fact, we were.

Many great feasts were had by the people and us. The people would make a half moon circle around the Buffalo, confusing them, and then charging them with much yelling and screaming. The Buffalo would sometimes run in a very bad direction, eventually trapping themselves, and going over a jump cliff.

GRIZZLY, THE SPIRIT BEAR

Most of the Buffalo would die or were crippled. The people would take away all they could carry, sometimes leaving great amounts of good meat. We knew where these places were and always checked them during our rounds. If the wind was right, we could smell a kill for many miles. There was so much to eat that sometimes, maybe a dozen of us shared the bounty, with only a few minor fights and squabbles.

After high water we feasted again, for the fish would get trapped as the water receded and leaving the fish in shallow pools. As the Buffalo traveled through our territory some would die of old age or sickness and many would hurt their legs in Prairie Dog towns. Of course, this was easy pickings for us and made good winter fat, as did the low water fish.

Occasionally, we would come across a fresh wolf kill. They tried to stand their ground, but they were no match for us. We would kill one now and then with our strong paws.

Once in a very great while, we would come across a fresh Mountain Lion kill. They didn't give it up very easy. Sometimes, we lost an eye or received other serious wounds from their swift claws. In the end, of course, we would run them off and enjoy their kill.

We really didn't kill many other large animals. Even with our great claws and fangs they could out run us so we couldn't strike.

Some of our huge old boars would learn to kill a moose. They would patrol the willows where the moose loved to feed. In this cover it was easy to stalk the moose and get very close.

GRIZZLY, THE SPIRIT BEAR

Those huge old boars could break a large bull Moose's neck with one swipe of their great paws.

With our great strength, we could drag a Moose from the willows to the timber. After feeding we would cover up the remains with limbs, brush, and debris. Then we would go lay down and watch over the kill until we wanted to eat some more.

We knew where the Elk and Deer gave birth to their young. Sometimes, we could find the young ones for an easy meal.

By far and large, we ate more grasses, sedges, nuts, and berries than anything else. Digging Ground Squirrels was more sport than anything else. Every once in a while, we would find a Bee's nest which we would rob with great relish.

In other words, we were great scavengers, and not the horrible killers that we have been called and named. Sometimes, we would pick a poor winter den or we had not fattened ourselves well enough for our winter slumber. Some of us would die before spring came.

By and large, living with the people was easy times for us and we often lived for more than twenty years. We were the gentle rulers of this land now called America.

GRIZZLY, THE SPIRIT BEAR

GRIZZLY, THE SPIRIT BEAR

CHAPTER TWO
ONE EYE THE SNAKE BEAR

The story of ole One Eye takes place on the plains near what is now Ogallala, Nebraska. He was born down, in what is now called the "Birdwood."

This is a deep canyon a few miles north of the North Platte River near the small town of Paxton, Nebraska. Many who live in that area don't even know that this canyon exists. A person comes upon it very abruptly in those sand hills without warning. In places it is several hundred feet deep with steep sides straight. A little stream runs through it with lots of trees and vegetation. To this day, it abounds with wildlife and strong natural growth.

One Eye's mother had dug herself a nice den on the North facing side of the Birdwood Canyon. Around December, One Eye, his sister, and his brother were born. They were about the size of a Tree Squirrel and awfully tiny compared to their giant of a mother.

The den was spacious and she easily moved them around until each offspring had a nourishing teat for their growth. Even with unopened eyes, they could easily find the source of that warm rich milk that was there for them. They grew like fat little butterballs on her rich milk and it wasn't long until their eyes had opened. Their mother scarcely moved during this time and they soon learned to crawl around in the dark den. After a few weeks they began playing and tumbling around together.

Then about the first week in March, a tiny light appeared at the top of the den entrance. The snow cover was melting. One Eye's brother was very curious and much bolder than the others. He crawled up and dug the entrance hole snow cover away until they could see outside into the very bright light. It hurt their little eyes.

The second week of March the mother came out of her slumber. She checked each cub carefully and would bathe them with her tongue, getting her moist scent all over them. She acted like most mothers, almost human-like, and she seemed very proud.

On the second day, she cleared the opening to the den the rest of the way, leaving the cubs inside. She climbed down the side of the Birdwood to the small stream. She was very hungry because her internal system had been shut down for many months during her slumber. She first took water and then ate some of the plants growing at the edge of the water. This nourishment started her internal systems working again. Soon, her bodily functions were operating as they should be, releasing everything inside of her.

At this point she was really hungry. She continued to eat more of the plants as she walked along the edge of the stream in hopes of finding something more substantial to eat. She worked her way close to a timbered area. There she found the remains of a fairly large bird which was sticking up out of the snow. It had been there all winter, but she ate it anyway, feathers and all.

GRIZZLY, THE SPIRIT BEAR

When she returned to the den, the cubs were outside playing in the snow. She managed to get them back inside and began feeding them once again.

The next day she took the cubs with her down to the water. They were now about the size of a large Marmot and packed full of energy. They tried the water but like most kids just ended up playing in it with their new found abandon and had a great time doing so. The mother Bear was also feeling better and a lot stronger from the nourishment of the plants and the rotten bird she had found.

Early the fourth morning after going down to the stream they left the den for the last time. She led them down the Birdwood to where the South side of the canyon wasn't so steep. A small animal trail led up over the top. Of course the cubs were having a time of it tumbling and sliding back down in the snow as they worked themselves to the top of the canyon.

The mother seemed in a hurry, getting a little rough with her offspring from time to time. They finally followed her over the top of the canyon and out into the snow-covered sand hills. Even with their newly opened eyes which weren't very good yet, they could see what seemed like a view of the plains that went on forever.

The mother Bear now headed due South and her cubs traveled along behind her as they covered a lot of ground at a remarkable rate. Late that afternoon they could see trees and a large river ahead. They had covered about twenty miles that day and were approaching the North Platte River. As they grew closer to the river, they could see brush and willows. There were large birds by the thousands along the river and in

GRIZZLY, THE SPIRIT BEAR

the air. Most of the birds were Sand Hill Cranes and their cries were almost deafening in their volume. There were some larger birds with black wingtips mixed in with the Sand Hill Cranes. These were Whooping Cranes which really stood out among the rest.

This spot was where the mother Bear was headed for she knew that there would be millions of migrating birds gathered there, many of which would be dead or crippled. She took her cubs over to a large stand of Cottonwoods. After having to scold One Eye's brother and chasing him back, she left them there while she started searching the willows along the riverside for food. She didn't have far to go when she found a dead crane washed up and entangled in the willows. This one she also ate feathers and all for her hunger was very great.

Soon she saw another of the great birds walking in the willows with its wing dragging. Perhaps it had been hit and wounded by one of the great Eagles that amassed there to also feed on the Sand Hill Cranes.

The mother Bear, not wanting to take any chances, eased into the water. The water was moving slowly and was only about three or four feet deep. This in turn covered most of her great bulk as she silently moved down-river until she was parallel with the wounded crane. She planted her back feet on the river bottom and came out of the water in a huge rush. The crane had no chance of escape and could only cower down as the mother Bear grabbed him with her paws. One bite to the crane's long neck and he was dead. This time the mother Bear removed some of the bird's feathers as she devoured it, getting the sweet taste the fresh meat and blood.

GRIZZLY, THE SPIRIT BEAR

When there was nothing left but a pile of feathers she left the river and returned to her cubs. The cubs, having been left outside for an extended period for the first time were somewhat fearful, came running with great excitement to meet their mother. With just that one good feed the mother seemed to have more milk ready and the cubs ate until they were as tight as a drum and ready to burst.

After the cubs had fallen asleep and darkness had been on the land for a while, the mother Bear left the cubs again, going back down to the river. The river was not just one main stream, but had many channels that were divided by islands. Some of these islands were no more than a barren sandbar. This is where the Sandhill Cranes and Whoopers would roost during the night.

The mother Bear had worked her plan for years with great success when the cranes were there. She knew that they would stay almost into May busy selecting their mates, until they headed on their journey far to the north.

The she Bear's plan was simple. She would go into the river, using one of the deeper channels where her bulk would be hidden. She would drift in the mild current until it carried her down to one of the islands covered with sand and birds. The birds were so thick that they resembled a solid object instead of many individual ones. The she Bear would charge into the mass of birds trying to get into the air. She struck with her mighty paws like lightning. Several of the birds were killed and many more were wounded before they could take flight. She searched for and killed the wounded that hadn't gotten into the water and escaped down-river.

GRIZZLY, THE SPIRIT BEAR

This charge had netted her ten birds. When she could get the wind at her back as she approached an island, she could get even more birds. The birds were heavy and had to fly into the wind to get airborne swiftly, thus flying right into the mother Bear.

The mother Bear now started eating on the first of her kill. She removed most of the feathers and ate until but one bird remained. Her sides were bulging and she was so full that she just wanted to lie there and sleep. But being the good mother that she was, she picked up the remaining bird and took it back to where her cubs were sleeping.

As she approached the trees where the cubs were, two of the cubs came running. The third cub was still asleep next to one of the big trees.

The bird's long neck had been dragging the ground. She dropped it next to the two cubs. The third cub came running and all three began to slowly approach the dead bird. They sniffed at it for a bit and gingerly reached out and touched it, not really knowing what exactly to do with it. As the mother Bear flopped down on her side, being full of her first large feed of the year, the cubs ignored the bird and went to her and fed on her rich milk until they all feel asleep once again.

Early the next morning the cubs were at the bird but only removing a few feathers as they played with it. Finally, the mother Bear woke up from her sleep. She came over and began removing the feathers from the bird. When she had gotten the bird down to mostly flesh, she began ripping small chunks of breast meat off and gave it to the cubs. Once again they played

GRIZZLY, THE SPIRIT BEAR

with it for quite a while until One Eye's brother finally ate his. The others soon followed suit and they had their first meal of meat.

Through the days that followed the mother Bear would continue to feed on the birds and bring some back for the cubs. They were now growing like weeds on their diet of milk and flesh.

They could now play almost all day, often wandering two to three hundred yards away from where their mother would leave them. They climbed trees, chased large insects, and once found a turtle that entertained them for most of one day as their mother slept nearby.

It was now getting close to May and the large birds were leaving in groups of mated pairs. Some would be traveling as far as the Arctic Ocean on their yearly journey. By now the mother Bear had regained all her weight that she had lost during the winter months as she slumbered. The cubs were now more than fifty pounds each and had become quite a handful for the mother bear to control.

The birds had begun their migration North. The mother Bear had to hunt longer and harder looking for dead or crippled birds. One day in particular while she was hunting, she came across an Elk carcass in the trees. Over half of the large animal was still there and they ate very well for about four days on the remains.

Most of the time now when the mother Bear would head off hunting in the mornings, the cubs would go exploring and playing. One day they were down by the river on a drift pile.

GRIZZLY, THE SPIRIT BEAR

By now the river had swollen due to the spring snow run off. The slow current was now very swift. One Eye's brother was jumping up and down on a log trying to make it go under the water when suddenly it broke lose from the tangled pile with One Eye's brother on top of it. The strong current caught the log and the young brother went down the river out of sight. He was now crying as loud as he could. The other offspring could hear him clearly, but there was nothing they could do, let alone know what to do. They did go down to the river bank for a few hundred yards, but soon came back to where their mother had left them.

When the mother Bear came back, she knew immediately that there was something wrong because the two cubs had a very frightened look in their eyes and were awfully quiet.

Using her great nose, she searched for the scent of the lost cub. The scent trail led her to the tangled drift pile and ended. At first she just walked back and forth on the large drift pile not knowing for sure what to do.

She then took the remaining cubs for miles down river searching as they traveled for her missing cub. They searched most of that day and eventually turned back until they had reached the drift pile again. The scent of her lost cub had grown faint and she became angry. In a flash she began tearing at the drift pile with her massive strength. Her great claws ripping and shredding at logs, branches, and limbs until there was nothing left except pieces of timbers, mangled branches, and debris floating in the swift current down the river for miles.

GRIZZLY, THE SPIRIT BEAR

They stayed in that general area for almost a week, but never saw the lost cub again. Finally, hunger forced them to leave and go in search of food. By now the Deer and Elk were having their young. The mother Bear knew where their calving grounds were at. She gathered up her two remaining cubs and took them to this place in the middle of the calving season.

It wasn't long after their arrival at the Elk calving grounds before the mother Bear found a newborn Elk calf hiding in the underbrush. The calf never moved an inch, not even a twitch. The calf only stared at the mother Bear's approach with those huge luminous brown eyes that seemed to open into the little Elk's soul. One well-placed bite to the little Elk calf's neck and it was dead. She then brought the cubs to the kill and soon they all had the Elk devoured.

They had plenty of food for a couple of weeks because it was fairly easy to get the Elk calves during the first two or three days of life. After the third day however, it was very hard to catch an Elk calf. By then, the calves could run like the wind.

By now the vegetation along the river was very lush. There were mushrooms and all kinds of treats to be found by the mother Bear and her cubs. They patrolled a stretch of river land that extended about twenty miles. Only now and then would they have the luxury of finding meat from a dead or crippled animal. Now and then they would catch a turtle laying out on a bank or frogs, or occasionally they would find a Beaver that had strayed a little too, far from the water.

They did see people from time to time, but would always hide in the thick river brush until they passed by. Other Bears would sometime pass their hunting grounds along the river. If

GRIZZLY, THE SPIRIT BEAR

the Bear was a male Grizzly, the mother Bear would swiftly herd her cubs away from him, putting a safe distance between them as fast as possible.

Soon it was the time of the berries. They would eat and play. Even the mother Bear joined in with the cubs. Sometimes, they all played until the day was done and they were exhausted. This was the best of the good times. They were all putting on weight rapidly now.

One morning they awoke to frost on the ground and the now slow moving waters of the river had a thin layer of ice on it. At that time the mother Bear took them away from the river bottom, going North, back toward the Birdwood. She knew where the people had their Buffalo jumps. Even a bluff of fifty feet would work for a jump site.

So far the cubs hadn't tasted Buffalo meat. As a matter of fact, they would hide in the underbrush when the huge thundering herds would come running to the river for water.

The mother Bear checked a few of the jump sites she knew about. All they found were bones from last year's kill. They resumed their trek North toward the Birdwood, to a site about ten miles East of where the old den was located.

They saw people coming from the direction of the jump site. They were loaded down with much Buffalo. The mother Bear and her cubs quickly flattened themselves out on the ground in a low spot and let the people pass by. They journeyed onto the jump site and arrived just before dark.

GRIZZLY, THE SPIRIT BEAR

They found the remains of many Buffalo. The hides and hindquarters had gone with the people. Most of the forequarters and entrails were still there, with a lot of carcasses to chew on from which they found good nourishment. This bonanza of hundreds of pounds of meat was hard to believe.

There was a spring nearby that was well hidden with brush. They used the hidden spring to quench their thirst and to hide in while they slept. They stayed there, eating and sleeping until the cold weather began to approach.

One evening, a pack of wolves approached the jump site. The mother Bear elected to depart the jump site, leaving the rest of the meat for the wolves, rather than getting her cubs hurt.

They spent days traveling the ten miles or so along the Birdwood river bottom heading toward the old den site. Along the way they would stop and eat fermented berries and other wild plains fruit. Sometimes they would get a little light headed and a pleasant feeling from eating the fermented delicacies.

A large storm was brewing in the distance. The mother Bear knew from her years of life experience what was in store and had been waiting for it. She knew it was time to head for the old den. As the flakes of snow were beginning to fall, she and the cubs increased their pace on their way to the old den. The old den was much the way they had left it. Some digging with her huge paws was required to enlarge the den before it would shelter the bulk of the fattened cubs and herself.

The cubs could still go outside for several days yet and play around the vicinity of the den. On the other hand, the

GRIZZLY, THE SPIRIT BEAR

mother Bear wanted to sleep all of the time. The next big snow approached and the cubs joined their mother in the den for the annual winter's sleep.

It was a very hard winter with heavy snow that year. The mother Bear and her cubs were oblivious to the harsh winter due to the large amounts of fat they had put on. The mother Bear had provided well for herself and her cubs. Her experience and the plentiful bounty of the plains had treated them well. Quite simply, they slept through the whole thing.

The mother Bear slept a week longer this year and didn't wake up until past the middle of March. She had to dig out their den entrance this time. As she and the cubs emerged, they slid half way down the South canyon wall. They went to the stream where they ate some water plants to purge their systems.

The mother knew she was running about a week late getting to the big river that year and the feast of Sandhill and Whooping Cranes. Sensing a need to push on, she led the cubs down-river to the familiar trail that led up out of the Birdwood. They found heavy drifts of snow in spots this year. While walking on top of them they would fall through and have to dig themselves out. It took them three hours to traverse the trail this year, where last year it only took them a few minutes.

They reached the North Platte River and as usual the birds were there in the millions. The mother Bear started bringing back crippled birds alive and the cubs soon learned how to kill their own food. One night she took the cubs with her on the river island bird hunt. As they approached the island filled with birds, one of the cubs, caught-up in the

GRIZZLY, THE SPIRIT BEAR

excitement of the hunt, jumped from the water early. The mother Bear had only managed to knock down one bird. When she was done scolding the young sow cub, both cubs knew that this bird hunting was a very serious matter.

They soon learned to go out on their own and make good kills. All three of them had gained back the weight they had lost during the winter months in the den.

When the birds were gone, they once again headed for the Elk calving grounds. The cubs learned how to take down a newborn Elk calf and kill it for food. Once, they even caught a calf that was over a week old because it had fallen in the brush while they were chasing it. This second or two was all they needed to catch the older calf. The cubs could now run almost as fast as a horse.

On another day they came across a cow Buffalo that had a broken back leg, probably from a prairie dog hole. The cow had come to water and would probably die there eventually. The cubs decided to attack this helpless looking Buffalo cow. One cub grabbed the good back leg of the cow and the other went for the neck. Ole One Eye sure got fooled that day for the Buffalo cow spun around quickly and hit him with her head, sending him flying more than ten feet. He was lucky he hadn't gotten gored by one of her stout horns.

The mother Bear joined in the fight. With the cubs having a hold of the back legs, she went for the head. Rearing up, she delivered a staggering blow with her giant paw to the cow Buffalo's head. The cow shuddered, her head turned from the blow. Then swiftly, the mother Bear bit down on the neck of the cow Buffalo and you could hear the distinct snap as the bones were broken. They ate this Buffalo and one other that they had taken from the wolves.

They followed the same routes and gorged on an over abundance of berries due to the heavy snows that year. They finished the year by fattening up on the berries. Once again, as they had last year, they trekked back to their den in the Birdwood for the winter.

In the spring, One Eye was the first to awaken. Maybe, it was getting rather crowded in the den this time around. The cubs had grown to about half the size of their mother, and she was kind of large herself.

One Eye dug out the entrance to the den the second week of March. He naturally headed down the South slope of the canyon. He was the first one to the stream this year. He ate some of the water plants to get his system working properly again. Now he was getting really hungry.

It still being early in the day, he headed West, upstream for a while. At one point, he came upon some fresh diggings in the stream bank. The heavy scent of Muskrat was in the air. He entered the little stream, blocking the freshly dug hole into the stream-bank. He commenced putting his heavy paws to work digging that Muskrat out. He dug about two feet and had it trapped, when the Muskrat tried to get past him. A bad mistake, for the muskrat almost ran right into the young Bear's jaws. That little morsel didn't really appease his inward groaning for food. It did however, give his stomach something to process.

GRIZZLY, THE SPIRIT BEAR

One Eye kept wandering up the stream until he was about five miles from the den. He found himself coming toward a large stand of trees. As he drew closer, he saw what were great claw marks on each of the first three trees in the stand. Puzzled, he reared up to take a closer look. Reaching only about halfway to the top of the great claw marks, his instincts became aroused. An uneasy feeling descended over him that he had never felt before. He didn't know what that it was all about, just knew it wasn't good. What he did know was that his mother had never taken him upstream from the den for some reason or another. He was really feeling restless and nervous now. He even thought he had heard something at the back of the stand of trees.

That did it. One Eye wasn't going stay around and find out whether he was right or not. He started running as fast as he could back down the stream. Talk about making tracks fast. After he had flown-low for about a mile, he slowed down and was feeling kind of foolish. He didn't know it then, but One Eye was in his father's territory up there by those trees that had those huge claw marks on them. It wouldn't have gone well for him if he was caught up there and it could have even cost him his life.

One Eye's father was in his prime at this time. He was about 12 years of age and was the largest of the Great Plains Grizzly Bears for more than a hundred miles in any direction. He weighed more than a thousand pounds and when he stood on his hind legs he towered close to ten feet tall. The Great Plains Grizzlies were larger than their brothers in the mountains, perhaps because they could stay out longer in the fall and come out of the den earlier in the spring. Getting extra days to feed was surely a bonus.

GRIZZLY, THE SPIRIT BEAR

One Eye returned to the den and found his sister awake. She had already been down to the stream for her water plants and system purging. The mother Bear was still asleep. His mother was in her eighteenth year now and on her third set of cubs. She seemed in good shape and maybe wanted to just sleep a little longer.

The mother Bear awoke the next morning with the cubs. She immediately went down to the stream to purge her system. This year she seemed a little indifferent toward her cubs and was rather cross when she headed off downstream to the game trail that led them annually out of the canyon.

This time they made good time getting across the sand hills and arrived at the North Platte River well before dark. The mother Bear found one crippled Sand Hill Crane hiding in the willows before dark. This time she did not share it with the cubs.

When darkness fell they had their last hunt together. They made a great kill together on the second island they tried. Something like fifteen birds were now dead on the island. They stayed there eating until daylight and the birds were all gone. Feathers lay strewn all about the island. The Bears hadn't even put a small dent in the crane population. Millions were now in the air making their loud and boisterous mating calls. The Bears finally left the island. They went into the trees at the river's edge to lie down for some sleep and give that huge meal a chance to settle.

Just about dark that evening One Eye awoke to find only his sister with him. He could see the depression in the grass where his mother had been laying. Looking around he

GRIZZLY, THE SPIRIT BEAR

realized she was gone. One Eye woke his sister and then he picked up his mother's scent trail. He and his sister followed it upriver. After about a mile or so the scent ended because his mother had gone into the river where she knew they wouldn't be able to track her. This she had done with all her cubs over the years.

They went several miles upriver that night. They were unable to find her scent again or where she had left the river and gone back onto land. They couldn't find a thing that would point them toward their mother. They even tried going into the river finding that there were three separate channels divided by islands. Their mother could have gone up any one of them.

One Eye and his sister returned to where they had slept the night before hoping somehow that their mother would have returned. There was nothing but the matted grass from where they had all slept before. They wandered around that area for close to two days and finally on the second night they decided that they needed to hunt. They caught five birds between them. They stayed around this productive area until the Sand Hill and Whooping Cranes had left for the North country.

They didn't know it, but their mother had gone up to join their father and work on another litter of cubs. This pregnancy would be her last. Their father hunted twenty miles upriver from where they were and the mother Bear found him the same day she arrived in his territory.

This huge Bear had learned to harvest the Buffalo that would get caught in the quicksand when they crossed the river in the wrong places. It seemed there was always a Buffalo caught in one or the other of the bad spots. You could count on it. The sand would make a tight suction on their legs and they would sink down to their bellies, hopelessly trapped. Just this three or four feet of quicksand was all that was needed to hold them until they would die.

Old Thor the giant Grizzly, which was One Eye's father's name, had learned just how far he could go out on the firm sand before he too would be trapped. From his spots of safety he could often reach the trapped Buffalo. He didn't care if they were dead or alive. As a matter of fact, he preferred the ones who had been dead a while. It was only a matter of one of his powerful bites to the back of the neck of the live ones, and their struggles were over.

The giant Grizzly Thor would brace his feet on the last of the firm sand. He would then latch onto the Buffalo's neck exerting a steady tension on the huge body of the Buffalo by pulling. His strength was enormous within his neck and shoulders and he would increase this tension when he felt any give of the buffalo's large body by the quicksand. This might go on for a couple hours, sometimes, until he would finally work the Buffalo carcass free of the quicksand. Only a couple of times did he ever have to leave one of the giant bull Buffalos stuck in the quicksand. Even then, he would still eat what he could reach of the bull from his position of safe footing on the firm sand.

This was the giant Bear's total hunt and the only extra things that he would eat were a little grass and berries when they were in season and had ripened. Most of the time you could find him laid out on one of his favorite bluffs, living the good life. He did expend a little extra energy during the mating

GRIZZLY, THE SPIRIT BEAR

season for he had at least three sows he bred each year on a regular basis if they were in season. Sometimes he had even more. Two of the sows with which he mated yearly would even come into his territory for mating. They were so impressed by his size.

So far Thor had never been challenged by another male Grizzly Bear. All he had to do was stand up to his full height and the other Bear was hightailing it for the willows.

One Eye and his sister went to the Elk calving grounds after the birds had left. They caught a few calves before the Elk herd moved on. The ties that held them together were breaking and growing thinner every day. One day the sister crossed the North Platte River and kept going South until she reached the South Platte River. It was only about three or four miles between the two rivers in this area.

One Eye ran across his sister's scent on only two or three occasions during his lifetime. He was now on his own. And for One Eye, like all male Grizzlies, he liked it that way. He would now only join up with another Bear during mating season.

One Eye was a digging Bear. He loved to dig. He would dig for Gophers, Prairie Dogs, and Racoons, you name it, he dug it. Of course, this was a waste of energy for what little meat it provided, but he sure enjoyed it none the less. The area he liked was always full of life and it wasn't hard for him to find something to eat just about anytime he wanted.

One day he was about twelve miles East, down the river from where he had learned to hunt birds. He stayed there a lot of the time now. On a little bluff near the river a family of

GRIZZLY, THE SPIRIT BEAR

racoons had their dens with several entrances. One Eye was digging in the lower entrance when he started up the bluff to the top hole. As he stuck his head over the crest of the bluff, a huge Prairie Rattlesnake sounded its warning. It was too late for One Eye to retreat. The Rattler struck him in the corner of his left eye in the soft tissue. One fang sank very deep and the other discharged venom into the skin near the eye. One Eye felt instant and intense pain like a lightning bolt had struck his eye. He fell over and rolled down the bluff trying to remove the pain with his paws. The swelling started very quickly because the rattler hadn't eaten in three weeks and he had given One Eye a full dose of his venom. Very rapidly, both of One Eye's eyes had swollen shut and he could no longer see at all.

One Eye tried running but he only fell over things. His nose still worked a little and he could smell the river, so he headed in that direction. He ran into the willows and forced himself through them to the water where he drank and stuck his head into the river which helped a little to ease the horrible pain. After drinking he pulled himself back into the willows. His suffering and pain had only begun. After only a couple of hours his whole head was about twice it's normal size. His throat was closing causing him to have a hard time breathing.

Finally he went into a blessed coma and lay there for two days gasping for air. On the third day he woke up to the same intense pain and he was still blind. He found the river again and drank a huge amount of water even though it was hard to get down his swollen throat. The inside of his mouth was black from the venom and his sense of smell was very weak now. He lay there for another day suffering, close to the water, so he could drink often. He had heaved up everything in his stomach

GRIZZLY, THE SPIRIT BEAR

and was getting the pangs of hunger on top of all this other pain.

On the fifth day, he started seeing a little light in his right eye and the swelling had gone down quite a bit. By the sixth day, he could see well enough from the right eye and tried walking. However, he ran into things because of the focus from having only one eye. It was like learning to walk all over again for the Bear.

The seventh day he was feeling better and was by now really hungry. His left eye had turned a milky white and would remain that way for the rest of his life. Just a sightless orb. His full sense of smell had come back and maybe even better than before.

One Eye started up river into the wind learning not to bump into things as he walked. After several miles he caught the scent of a Mule Deer that had washed up under a drift pile. It had tried to cross the river during the spring snow runoff and had drowned in the high water. He was very lucky to have found this Deer. He started tearing apart the drift pile until he could clamp onto the neck with his jaws. He was almost full grown now and had a lot of that great strength that only Grizzlies possess. He pulled the Deer out of the pile and up onto the bank. It was bloated from being dead several days. The air escaping from the stomach made funny hissing noises as he ripped it open to get at the liver.

One Eye fed until he was just about as bloated as the Deer had been. Not wanting to take any chances, he stretched himself out across the Deer's carcass and went to sleep. This was the first day in a week that the pain was not so great from

GRIZZLY, THE SPIRIT BEAR

the Rattler's bite. He stayed there for another day and finished off the Deer carcass.

Other than his faulty vision, he was in pretty good shape for what he had been through. It has been said that animals don't know things like hate and love, but this Bear now hated rattlesnakes. As you have probably guessed, his disposition toward Rattlesnakes wouldn't improve for the rest of his life.

The berries were now getting ripe. He feasted on them and also ate a little grass. The urge for meat came on ole One Eye and he headed for one of the Buffalo jumps that his mother had shown him as a cub.

The second Buffalo jump site he checked had been used by people. They had only killed about six Buffalo at this jump site and there was very little meat left over from other animals. He did get some neck meat and the remains of some entrails. Even the heads had some good meat on them. He spent his second day there removing the head meat. It was a hard job and took a lot of time for what little meat you could scavenge in return.

One Eye now headed back toward the East where the bluff country was located which was near to where that Rattler had bitten him. His mother had taught him about Rattlesnakes and that it was better to leave them alone. However, his hatred of them overrode everything she had taught him and he began looking for them. He knew they would soon be heading for their dens for the winter and better yet, he knew where several of these den sites were located.

GRIZZLY, THE SPIRIT BEAR

One Eye was about a mile from the first den site when he heard the familiar sound of a rattle from under some bushes near him. He was very careful as he circled the bushes until he could make out where the snake was hiding. As he circled the bushes, the snake would turn his head and follow his every move. The urge to kill that snake was mounting in One Eye. He knew it wasn't the one that had bit him before. He really didn't care. It was a Rattlesnake and that was good enough for him.

Finally, he slapped at the snake with his massive paw, the snake struck at him but missed by a foot. Again, he struck and some of the brush fell and pinned the snake to the ground. He then smacked at the snake with his other paw, wounding and stunning it to the point that it was almost dead. He ripped and tore at the brush, throwing the snake, brush, and all out in the open where he could clearly see it. The snake could hardly move its head as One Eye jumped on it with both front paws, successfully pounding it into the ground. When he had finished his tirade, only half of the snake remained. Half was turned to mush. The first half he promptly ate. He found it to be pretty good eating.

One Eye then began circling the toward the den. He was a mile away from it and worked his way slowly inwards. Each circle smaller, ever closer to the den. He found six more Rattlesnakes while doing this. He carefully killed and ate them. The third snake he killed had bitten him on the paw, causing it to swell-up a little, but didn't seem to bother him much. His system had built up a resistance to the venom due to how severe his first encounter with a Rattler had been. As he moved onto another den, he killed over a dozen more Rattlers.

GRIZZLY, THE SPIRIT BEAR

They had their own layers of winter fat on them and this was in turn, putting weight on him.

One Eye's sense of smell was very acute now and he could track a Rattler's scent for miles. They had an odor about them that kind of smelled like cucumbers. He tracked the Rattler's scent and found more dens that way. The first frost had come and the Rattler's were almost all in the dens or laying out close to them during the warm days. Even with them being slower from the cooler weather, a few would manage to strike One Eye on his paws. Only a little pain was felt by the big Bear and he exuberantly killed many.

At one particular Rattlesnake den site, he found that the rock in that area was a soft sandstone. He soon found that his claws could dig it away. He started digging and rolling rocks down the hillside until he had broken into the den area. There were dozens of Rattlers in there and they were cold and couldn't even strike at the their angry intruder. One Eye took advantage of the situation. He had a great feast eating Rattlesnakes and stayed there three days until he had eaten them all.

It was late Fall now, almost winter. One Eye's driving force became the urge to find a den site of his own. The first snow was starting to fall as he trekked back towards the Birdwood and the den he had been born in. When he arrived at the den site, he could see a little steam coming out of a tiny opening on top of the entrance to the den. He knew that his mother would be in there and he also knew that he would not be welcome.

GRIZZLY, THE SPIRIT BEAR

One Eye turned down the canyon wall and went to the stream and looked West. He remembered the big claw marks very high up on those trees. He turned and went East down the Birdwood, often climbing up the canyon's sides checking for likely den sites along the way. Nothing seemed to look right to him. As he journeyed on, going about ten miles until he spotted a ledge up on the South side of the Birdwood. The climb up was difficult and steep, but the digging was rather easy. Somehow he knew how to do this as all Bears do. His instincts kicked-in as he worked on his new den site. He made the entrance tunnel as narrow and small as possible and still be able to get in there and remove dirt. He'd have to squeeze his large body in and out as he removed the dirt from inside the nice cavity that he was preparing for winter. When the den was finished, he fooled around down at the stream. He ate what fermented berries he could find. When the big snow came, he tucked himself in for his first winter's sleep alone.

One Eye's internal clock must have been set for the middle of March because he awoke from his slumber as usual for the Birdwood's Bears. It took him a while to dig out the entrance to the den because the snow was heavy again that winter. He slid down the slope in places that were steep to the stream. He kind of enjoyed it. It reminded him of way that he, his sister, and his brother had played. He ate the water plants and purged his system, getting ready for his first full year of hunting alone.

The next day he found a trail up over the Birdwood and headed across the Sand Hills to the North Platte River. He had been generally heading West so that he would hit that part of the river where he had learned to take Sandhill Cranes.

GRIZZLY, THE SPIRIT BEAR

Again this year, they were there by the millions. Their loud calls could be heard for miles. They flew so high that it was hard to see them as they traveled on the upper thermal winds for hours at a time. One Eye made the usual patrols along the river bank in the willows until he found a Whopping Crane with a broken wing. This bird was huge and could look down on him. He tried to fight off the Bear as he was attacked. The Whopping Crane had no chance and soon One Eye had him by the neck and it was over. This was the first time he had eaten one of those big, mostly white birds and decided it was about the same as the others.

That night he made a island raid on the birds and somehow his sight threw him off some. He didn't get a kill on that first island. He was really careful on the next island and got six birds after killing the cripples.

He was there about a week. Every day he was eating his fill and putting on good weight. One day as he was sleeping in the willows when he heard a sound that woke him up. It was his mother charging him and she looked damn serious. There were two little cubs behind her trying to keep up. One Eye bolted out of there, running for his life. He soon outdistanced her and the new cubs. So much for a mother's love.

He moved from there down river about eight miles until he found the good type of islands with bare sand and deep water along side for good ambush approaches. He stayed there until the birds left, gaining back all his weight from the winter's losses. He had a taste for Elk, but was now afraid to go where his mother might be hunting with the cubs. Instead he crossed the North Platte River and headed East on the South side of the

GRIZZLY, THE SPIRIT BEAR

river until he found a calving ground. There he ate well for about two weeks and then the Elk left.

He hadn't forgotten about the Rattlesnakes, especially every time he bumped into something on his blind side. He crossed back over the river and headed for the snake den areas that he hunted last year. Sure enough, they were starting to come out of their dens and he caught and killed many dozens of them. He was situated in a cool place that couldn't be seen until you were just above it. Down in this little canyon that he had found was a large grove of trees and a running spring at the head of it. One Eye loved to lay by the gurgling water and have his Bear dreams.

One day, while he was there in his favorite place, he was startled awake by a crashing sound in the trees and brush. A small five point Elk, still in his velvet almost ran over him laying there. He lunged up from his bed of grass and grabbed the Elk by the throat and pulled it down. His bite shut off the Elks air supply. He held it firmly until it died. He found that the young Elk had an arrow embedded deep inside its back by the last two ribs and high up. The Elk had been trying most of the day to elude the one who had shot him. Even with a minimal lose of blood, the hunter was still tracking him. The Elk had bled on the inside as most high wounds will do.

One Eye had just started to open the Elk up when he heard a sound. It was the hunter and he was standing only a few feet away. Usually the people wouldn't bother a Grizzly Bear and stayed away as best as they could. However, this was a young brave of about seventeen years and he wanted his Elk. The brave hesitated out of respect for the Bear. He then noticed the great milky white eye and it spooked him. He fired

GRIZZLY, THE SPIRIT BEAR

an arrow at close range and hit One Eye in the shoulder. The arrow head hit bone and didn't go in very far. This hurt One Eye almost as much pain wise as that first Rattlesnake bite had. One Eye charged the brave with rage in his heart. The brave didn't have time to notch another arrow. He threw down his bow and ran for the nearest tree. It was a bad choice of trees for the brave with limbs only about six feet off the ground. He climbed through the first set branches, reaching the next set. At this point, it should be noted that Grizzlies also climb trees. One Eye went right on up that tree after the young brave.

The brave thought he was safe, but One Eye reached his foot and clamped down with his powerful jaws. He literally yanked that young brave down through the limbs of that tree. He mauled that young brave savagely with a rage that came from being wounded. He quit and walked off, leaving behind him the death body of the would-be hunter. Suddenly, One Eye turned and once more mauled the young brave's lifeless corps before he finally departed for good.

One of the brave's friends had been hunting with him and had finally caught up to the young brave as he was being dragged from the tree. He witnessed the quick death of his friend. The brave ran back to his camp and it wasn't long before the story of "Ole One Eye" grew among the tribes of people. They did not seek revenge on One Eye. Instead, he became more like a Spirit Bear to them. He was talked about much at the camp fires. The people often saw One Eye killing the Rattlesnakes. The legend of One Eye grew even larger among the people.

One Eye lived for twenty-four years and only mated twice with the same sow. People thought this was because of his

GRIZZLY, THE SPIRIT BEAR

one milky white eye and that the sows were spooked at his appearance when he came courting.

The Great Plains Grizzlies had a real good life in those days. They only needed a small area to live well and grow the fat needed to get through the harsh winters. This is not like the Grizzlies of today. Because of man, they need a much larger area for their survival. They sometimes hunt over hundred miles to just find enough food to survive. Food that use to be so plentiful.

GRIZZLY, THE SPIRIT BEAR

CHAPTER THREE

CROSSING THE GREAT RIVER

The big river was kind of a separation line for us Grizzly Bears. In fact, only a few of us lived East of the big river. We were like our local people and lived mostly off the Buffalo when it came to meat. When the strange people started showing up from the East beyond the big river, our numbers were around one-hundred thousand strong. The Buffalo numbered more than sixty million along with several million Elk.

What a truly good living system we had and life was abundant everywhere. You could walk all day long and never reach the other side of some of our Prairie Dog towns. There were millions of Sage Chickens and other birds, and many Antelope and Mule Deer. Almost every little range of hills had Bighorn Sheep living on them. In the very high country there were white goats.

The Wolves and Coyotes and other meat eaters numbered in the many thousands. Yet, they couldn't make a dent in the populations of grass eaters, except to not let them get out of hand. It was as it should be.

The people were many thousands strong and lived in small groups or tribes. They always respected the land and the life that were sustained by it. They would follow the Buffalo across these great plains and hills.

All of this was about to change forever. The goodness and balance of nature that was respected and worshiped by the people who lived here was about to come to an abrupt and

GRIZZLY, THE SPIRIT BEAR

tragic end. As these strange and different people started showing up from East of the big river, they brought with them a new way. That way was overindulgence, greed, and selfishness.

GRIZZLY, THE SPIRIT BEAR

CHAPTER FOUR
THE MOUNTAIN MEN

The first of the strange people to show up in our land were called the mountain men. They were pale in appearance and had hair on their faces. Their clothes and smell were also different from the people.

What was to eventually effect us the most about these strange people were the "fire-sticks." They always carried them everywhere they went. We saw them kill Elk and Deer at more than a hundred long walking steps. And much to our displeasure they started killing us with those fire-sticks as well. We would hear a loud sound and much smoke would come from the ends of those fire-sticks. Sometimes before we could hear or see these fire-sticks, we would be struck by a white-hot little ball they called lead. Many of us were killed by these little balls of lead. Many more were wounded or even worse, crippled to die a slow horrible death.

We had never known fear before nor been the hunted. The people or tribes rarely if ever hunted us. This was all new to us. Sometimes, we would charge them when they only wounded us. Some of them died in our attacks. Many were left marred and crippled wishing they had died. We left them with a reminder of the great strength we welded which heretofore we used only to hunt or defend ourselves with.

As the strange people moved deeper into our land, we got to know them better. A kind of respect grew for them or then again, maybe it was just the start of our learning the meaning of fear. Now we had to watch where we were going and to stay on the alert most of the time. Often we would feed on the remains of their kills. They would only take what they called the best parts of an animal for themselves, wasting great amounts of meat.

The people had never left us with much for they used all of the parts of an animals they killed. Unless that is, it was a huge kill at a jump site which was more than they could use and take with them.

Those first strange men didn't kill in what you would call a wanton manner. It was just the fact that they didn't eat all of what they had killed that puzzled us. Maybe it was the fact that they could carry only so many of those little lead balls and bags of black powder with them when they came into our land and didn't have room for the meat.

They also carried traps of steel which they used to catch and kill Beavers with. They never ate the Beaver, but only took its fur. We sometimes could catch a Beaver when they had to travel a long distance between the water and the trees they used for their dams. Most of the time, they would slam the water with their tails, making a loud slapping sound which warned the rest of their little community that danger was near.

These strange men would skin the Beavers they caught and leave the bodies with lots of fat on them. Some of us learned to follow them around as they worked their trap-lines so we could get easy meals of Beaver.

Usually there would be two of these strange men working the trap-lines together. When they would both leave their camp, we would often raid it. What great fun for they had tasty new foods, plus some we already had a taste for.

GRIZZLY, THE SPIRIT BEAR

They had bacon and a white powder called sugar, which were new, and honey which we loved but didn't have work for to get.

In retrospect, our raids on their camps were probably a mistake of great proportions for they started hunting us in a most serious manner. Most of the strange men had learned the ways of the people. They were good hunters and stalkers. Often, many of us were killed by them.

We saw these strange men get into fights with the people and many would die. We couldn't understand this for when we would fight amongst ourselves, we usually stopped before anyone was seriously hurt. This was part of the reason why we called them "strange." You see, wherever they went, needless death would surely follow.

Even with the voluminous killing they did, it hardly put a dent in the population of wildlife in those days. They grew in their knowledge of our land, learning the people's ways. As it turned out, this was to be our downfall. Very soon, they brought many, many others of their kind.

GRIZZLY, THE SPIRIT BEAR

CHAPTER FIVE
THE BUFFALO HUNTERS

Many of us were still left and roaming the Great Plains when the great slaughter of the Buffalo began. These hunters carried better and more efficient "fire-sticks." They could shoot more accurately and for longer distances. Distances of hundreds of yards. Now we were sure we had learned fear. Quickly we became fearful of these strange men for they seemed to have an endless supply of lead or what they called bullets. They would come for short periods of time. They stayed only long enough to fill their wagons with Buffalo hides which they would haul out to the other strange people East of the big river.

We and the people couldn't understand why they would kill a perfectly good Buffalo and take only the hide. Not to mention killing so many of them and leaving all that good meat to go to waste. The slaughter was beyond belief with all the thousands of Buffalo carcass's laying to rot in the sun. We ate what we could, but most just went to waste. Even the Wolves and Buzzards couldn't clean up this massive scene of death.

Very often, one of these Buffalo hunters would kill more than a hundred Buffalo in one stand. The Buffalo seemed to get confused, just standing there or milling around in one area. Maybe, they couldn't understand this outrage of so much wanton killing.

By this time we had learned well the true meaning of fear. Many of us that were left made a strategic decision to leave the Great Plains for the Rocky Mountains. The Elk were also slaughtered and those that were left soon followed us into the mountains looking for a safe refuge as well. By this time, our numbers had been cut in half as they killed us by the thousands. Instead of being rulers of the Great Plains, we became as the Coyotes, hiding and fearing for our lives.

GRIZZLY, THE SPIRIT BEAR

CHAPTER SIX
THE IMMIGRANTS

The bottom fell out of the Beaver market. Some of the trappers became guides, leading hordes of other strange people into our land. They were like earthworms after a rain. They just kept surfacing every time you looked.

What very few of us that were left hiding on the Great Plains could see wagons pulled by oxen and horses. These strange men brought their women and children with them. We saw many graves where many of them hadn't made it. Some died of the hardships while others were killed by the people or each other.

Many battles were fought between the people and the strange people with many dying in these fights. The people knew as we did, that our way of life was coming to an end never to return. We and the people fought as hard as we could, but was no match for their fire-sticks and numbers. There was much harm done to us.

Again, these strange people looked a lot like the people, but with ways that were vastly different. They brought diseases that the people had never known. Many of the people died of these illnesses. They brought with them what the people called firewater which caused havoc and destruction and also killed many of the people.

Many of the strange people broke off from the rest that were moving to the West and stayed on the Great Plains and foothills of the Rocky Mountains, building their homes and camps there. They were called settlers and ranchers. They

GRIZZLY, THE SPIRIT BEAR

would soon destroy most of our plush hunting grounds by digging them up with their steel tools and putting fences across the land.

GRIZZLY, THE SPIRIT BEAR

CHAPTER SEVEN
THE SETTLERS AND RANCHERS

There was a saying going around during these days, "dumb as a Buffalo." They may have lacked smarts in some areas, but the Buffalo and the people knew that digging up the prairie and hoping for crops were a very stupid venture. The strange people's government it seems had duped most of them with promises of free land if they went West.

No one can truly own the land you know. It was made only to live upon and then be buried in. It is still being proven to this day that a great mistake was made. It was a mistake to have put the plow to those spacious tall grass prairies. Now the water is running off and eroding the soil. The soil is dying from the lack of natural nutrients and requires great amounts of fertilizer to grow anything. It is now being found that the Buffalo had a meat that was far more nutritious and healthy than the cattle that the ranchers covet so much. So the Plains were dug up and the Buffalo replaced with those stupid domestic cattle that need lots of care.

These strange people had many foolish ideas that didn't fit well with the land. Some of our last few Bears on the Great Plains would raid the gardens that the strange people put in near to the mountains. It did taste good, kind of different, that is when they could actually get anything to grow. The people were growing desperate now and the wars took many causalities from both sides. The little homesteads were raided and also the large ranches that had brought in those stupid cattle from Mexico. It seemed everyone had a fire-stick in those days. They were coming into the rough country where we still had a few Bears trying to holding out.

GRIZZLY, THE SPIRIT BEAR

The ranchers and settlers waved about little pieces of paper that they called a deed to the land that their government had given them. How in the hell could they even start to claim this land that belonged to the people and us forever. It has always been that way. The people had lived on this land for many thousands of years without even leaving a dusty track to show that they had been there.

Our numbers now were very few. There were so many strange people around that it wasn't hard for them to find our tracks and sign. Not even a few of us were allowed to live near where the strange people lived. This was the fate of the Wolf, Coyote, Bob Cat and other animals. Prices were put on our heads and the end of our way and kind was coming very fast. Even the people were being rounded up and moved from the good land. Some were even being shipped back across the big river like the cattle the strange people brought here. What a trade, huh?

GRIZZLY, THE SPIRIT BEAR

CHAPTER EIGHT
THE BOUNTY HUNTERS

It seemed to us that it would be impossible for the strange people to kill all of us, along with the Buffalo and the Wolves. But they almost made it a reality.

The bounty hunters came for us in large numbers at first and they killed a few of us. So we retreated into even rougher country to survive. There was no mercy shown to us by these strange people. They would use huge steel traps that they would set to trap our legs and feet until they came back to kill us. The few of us that were caught suffered greatly before a welcomed death was delivered by the bounty hunters. These people became stranger each time a new wave of them appeared. They didn't get many of us this way because it was hard to carry very many of these huge heavy traps into the rough country.

They had smaller steel traps that they used on the wolf and many died suffering in great pain. Also, they would put out their poison baits that killed every living meat-eater that came across it including Eagles, Hawks, Ravens, Skunks, Possums, and Minks to name a few.

The bounty hunters finally left the area and gave up when the pickings became slim and the profits low. The wolves were almost gone and only a few of us Bears remained, hiding in the roughest and most remote of the terrain on the Great Plains.

GRIZZLY, THE SPIRIT BEAR

CHAPTER NINE
RAILROADS, TOWNS, & CITIES

When the railroad came across the prairies, it meant the end to a way-of-life. A way-of-life that the land had known since day one. Now, building supplies and heavy equipment were being brought in that could tear up the land at an alarming rate.

Special railroad cars or coaches were designed and put into service on the railroad lines for the rich so-called hunters, enabling them to shoot Buffalo in the luxury and comfort for which they were accustomed. The Buffalo would come up to the railroad tracks and just stand there, never having seen such a thing that just stretched across the land from horizon to horizon. They called it sport hunting. Some sport, huh?

The way was paved for these mass-murderers to shoot from the comfort of their coaches until the barrels of their rifles were too hot to touch. The helpless Buffalos would drop and pile like cordwood. They neither bothered skinning the many thousands of Buffalo corpses, nor take the tongue or hump for food.

We Bears certainly didn't benefit from the wanton killing either since we were already gone, having been driven from our homelands. Only the buzzards were left and could have their fill. That was even more than they could consume before the meat rotted and dried up in the sun.

I'm sure there must have been a few of the people there who witnessed this incredible slaughter with tears in their eyes, and a deep sorrow and anguish in their hearts. There is no doubt in our minds, that the Creator will somehow punish those who participated in this great murder of the Buffalo herds.

Now that the trains were there to haul freight, the strange people would gather the bones of the Buffalo and pile them up in large mountainous heaps. Most of these piles were higher than the few trees that were left and we think they used them for fertilizer and soap of some kind.

To give you some idea of the awesome destruction, and the waste of living creatures, simply multiply sixty million Buffalo by fifteen-hundred pounds each. You will come up with enough meat to feed every meat eater on the face of the earth many times over.

The number of strange people really began to surge due to the railroad tracks that could bring them across the prairies in such a short period of time. They came like hordes of Locusts, settling on the land with their little pieces of paper called deeds in their hands. Do you think perhaps, that they thought they could even get deeds to the sunrise and sunset?

Now that the strange people numbered in the hundreds of thousands, they started building permanent towns in the places that water could be found. The people could not understand a village that could not be moved. They had always followed the Buffalo and would pick good spots to hunker-down in to endure the harsh winters.

Hunting parties went out from these towns and cities and everything with hair or feathers was slaughtered. They even found a few of us hiding in the rough country.

GRIZZLY, THE SPIRIT BEAR

Our hides and those of the wolf, would be hung on the sides of the buildings in these towns and cities. We were now becoming what they called trophies. All those who claimed to be great hunters had to have some of our hides and remains around their homes. It soon took the strange people longer and longer trips to find anything to shoot at. Sometimes they came back without any trophies at all. Now, they began to worry, and much talk was going on in the little stores and bars.

The idea of seasons to hunt and bag limits were discussed. Finally, these laws were drawn up and passed in 1876. They didn't do this out of care or compassion for the animals, but so that the game would come back again for their own pleasure.

We knew that not all of these strange people were involved in the slaughter. Some only wanted a fair hunt and to enjoy the meat at their tables. Elk meat was far better than those rangy ole Longhorn cattle anyway.

GRIZZLY, THE SPIRIT BEAR

CHAPTER TEN
SPORT HUNTERS

Now that the animals on the plains and small hills were decimated, the strange people wanted more it seemed. Those able to afford it, and there were many, got together in large hunting parties with many pack horses, lots of comfort items, expensive food, and cooks to prepare it for them.

These great hunting parties would sometimes stay out for months at a time, and it seemed they mostly wanted the larger animals with horns or antlers so they could mount them on walls of their homes. The people and we Grizzlies, could never understand the taking of these animals for trophies. Even when the best of the taxidermy work was done, those glass eyes were dim reminders of what they used to be. Poignant in the fact that those glass eyes had a noticeable and total absence of the spirit and life that were once contained therein.

Even after the strange people had instituted seasons and bag limits, many of them didn't obey these laws. They continued to kill the animals like in the old days. Finally, what they called Game Wardens were put into place to enforce these laws. But many of them were corrupted by money and gold anyway.

By this time our only holdout was deep in the Rocky Mountains where the Elk had also come along with us. We had become mountain animals instead of what we born to be, animals living on the fruitful plains with the Buffalo. We were kind of holding our own, because the mountains offered many good hiding places where even the great hunting parties couldn't reach us. Over time we did suffer many losses. The good food available in the mountain's valleys kept our numbers somewhat in line, but nowhere near what they had been on the Great Plains.

On the other side of the great mountains ranges, near the great sea, the strange people would capture us alive and put us into pens. And not only did we have to live in pens, but they would make us fight dogs, wild cattle, and each other. For that matter, anything else their sick minds could find to use for their ugly sport. This was so they could have some kind of sick fun to satisfy their blood lusts and have their abusive fun with this abhorrent sport.

One of those great hunting parties was headed for the Yellowstone basin and had with it the Chief of the strange people. His name was Teddy Roosevelt. This man was a fine hunter and loved the beauty of the wilderness as we did. When he saw the country around the Yellowstone with its many geysers and stark beauty, with an abundance of wildlife, he knew that he had to preserve all this somehow.

When he went back across the mighty river, he began a big fight to protect and preserve this land by calling it a National Park. This National Park was to be there forever and was to be a place for us to have permanent refuge. He did accomplish this and we believe he saved us from going the way of the passenger pigeon and many others that became only a picture in a book.

Even with their laws of no killing in a National Park, many strange people still broke that law, killing animals like the wolf, who was completely decimated. They were killed down to the very last one.

GRIZZLY, THE SPIRIT BEAR

CHAPTER ELEVEN
HUNTERS IN GENERAL

As might be expected, we Grizzlies have given the hunters hell in this, the story of our lives. It is a well-known fact that the hunters did kill us off and abuse our freedoms, and guess what? They are still doing it today, but only on a smaller scale.

To set the record straight as best we can, after those game laws went into effect, it wasn't enough to save or increase the animals back to the way they were before the strange people showed up. The hunters had to start paying fees' for licenses and they were taxed on all hunting items they bought. This money was used by the appointed game commissions for wardens' wages, wildlife restoration, and wildlife protection.

Many animals came bouncing back from what looked like sure extinction like the Whitetail Deer, Elk, Turkey, Bighorn Sheep, and many more were given a new lease on life by the hunters and the fees they have paid over years, plus some environmental agencies came into the picture. This has been going on for more than a hundred years now and they have built up populations of most game animals which enables their being hunted. Of course until recently, we Bears and Wolves still caught hell and were considered predators and enemies of the strange people so we enjoyed no protection. That all has changed now and the strange people aren't allowed by law to shoot us. It still happens however because some of these strange people just won't listen and don't really care to. They aren't hunters they are just outlaws in the woods with guns.

GRIZZLY, THE SPIRIT BEAR

A good hunter knows what's around him in the woods and would rarely come close to us. He knows that our sows with cubs will fight to the death to protect their young from even a perceived threat, as well they should. Hell, most of us are fearful if not afraid of the strange people and we will run away if given the chance. We'll even bluff and give a false charge at the strange people to get them to run if possible. We are willing to share the wilderness, or what little of it that is left with the strange people. After all, it was ours first, and we have a right to live in this world too.

There are many groups now that want to stop the hunting all together. They know about all of the bad things that have happened to the animals. But, they are also so ignorant and sheltered from wilderness life that they don't even know what it's all about, even that things die in the natural order of things, even by hunters. There is a balance to nature endowed by the Creator. The food chain requires the death of some animals. Abuse of this order is another matter, but the two should not be confused.

When the strange people go to their Super Markets, they buy the red meat they find there that is doctored to be a bright and pleasing red color. I wonder where they think it came from, some man in the back of the counter that puts pills into water and "wallah" they have steak. It doesn't work like that, does it? Something has to die to make those steaks.

Lets take the case of "Billy the Bull" cow. He was born in March and the weather was very bad out there in the fields. His mother had a hard time because she was bred to a bull that was too large and the rancher wanted Billy to be much larger than his mother. Soon he was taken from his mother never to see her again. Next, they cut off his testicles and branded him with a red-hot iron, putting him through awful pain and trauma.

Billy now is shipped to a feed yard in a truck jammed with others like him. This feed yard is often knee deep in mud and cow dung with no where to go and no fresh graze to be found, only baled and dried hay. Just jammed again against each other waiting to get fat.

When he has reached the required weight, he is then crammed into a cattle truck, jammed shoulder to shoulder with his other condemned companions, for his last long journey to the slaughter house yards. Now he is put in an even nastier pen to gain back the weight lost that the trip has taken off of him. There he could smell the stench of death coming from the buildings as his buddies are led off to their deaths. Soon it was Billy's turn. Cattle ready for the slaughter. Ever wonder where that term came from? Not much of a life for Billy the Bull I'd say.

Lets now take a look at "Rudy the Elk." He was born in early May on the flats below the mountains. Rudy had many companions and they would romp and play enjoying being alive with the herd. Of course one or two of us Bears were always around looking for dinner. Hoping to get a chance at them. Rudy's mother and the other cow Elk took him and his friends across the river and headed into the high country shortly after they were big enough to feast on the greenery that was growing there. They stayed up in the high country where the bugs were few and the eating was great. Rudy had a beautiful time that summer and was growing like a weed.

GRIZZLY, THE SPIRIT BEAR

Fall came to the high country with its different type of beauty and soon after the snow started falling. When the snow got more than two feet deep, the Elk cows started moving the herd back to the low country and their winter feeding grounds. Of course the big Bull Elk had been around and kept the herd together until all had been bred for that season. Rudy had watched all of this and knew somewhere deep down inside that someday that this would be his position.

Rudy had heard these strange loud noises and he noticed that some of the Bulls would just drop to the ground and never get up. Even some of the cows and calves would do the same thing from time to time upon hearing the strange loud noises. Rudy's mother had been through this before. She knew where to hide and which way to come out of the high country to avoid the noise and the orange hunters. Rudy made it to the winter feeding grounds that year and he remembered all that he had seen, especially the routes they had taken to get there.

Rudy made this trip five more years, growing up to be the herd bull and a monarch of the mountains. His rack of antlers were huge and he fathered many sons and daughters. The Fall of his sixth year he was bugling and rounding up his harem of cows in a small meadow. He saw a flash of orange at the edge of the timber, but it was too late. He never even heard the noise that came after the shot.

The hunter who had shot Rudy didn't mind getting blood all over him. He knew where the fine steaks came from and what had to be done. He even stopped for a minute and payed homage to the heavens, profusely thanking the Creator for allowing him to harvest such a fine bull Elk.

GRIZZLY, THE SPIRIT BEAR

So, who had the better life? Billy or Rudy? This question is going to have to be answered as the move to stop hunting all together grows stronger. The State of Wyoming has a game and fish budget of about sixty million dollars a year that the hunters are paying. Who will pay to keep our wildlife safe and managed if the hunters are stopped?

The strange people as well as the people are meat eaters and as long as this is so perhaps hunting is the best way for many. Because death is hidden in a slaughter house doesn't mean, it never happened. Ask Billy. At least Rudy had a good life of several years in which he passed on his genes to many a fine Elk. Yes, ranchers need to make a living and city folk need to have a store, but we don't need to provide torment, pain, and bad conditions for any animal. To my way of thinking, there are better ways.

GRIZZLY, THE SPIRIT BEAR

A ONCE PROUD GRIZZLY NOW IN DEFEAT.

CHAPTER TWELVE
THE LAST STAND

We Grizzlies are intertwined in this hunting issue and our numbers are way too small to be allowing open seasons on us once again. The only stronghold in this country that we have left now is the Yellowstone National Park and the surrounding lands.

We are being shot as we come out of the Yellowstone National Park during bad food years to look for food to eat. We need room to travel the fringes of the park and expand our numbers without being shot by ranchers and those hunters who are not really hunters.

The ranches, for the most part, are owned by corporations, foreign big business, and wealthy people like movie stars. The cattle they run near the park, which admittedly we occasionally eat, are merely play things. The corporation ranches are used as tax write-offs while the rich individuals are just playing at rancher. There may be a few of the generational ranches around owned by the great grandson's of the ones who started them. Mostly, these ranches have been forced to be sold by the tax man.

Many of the ranches around now have dude ranch operations. They make more money from this than the few cattle they run. The dudes and all the people that come to Yellowstone have one thing in common, they want to see a Bear, even a Black Bear. This is their park and they deserve it to be as it was when Teddy Roosevelt set it aside for them forever. This means Grizzlies, Black Bears, and the Wolf, who by the way, is making a strong comeback even if they are still

GRIZZLY, THE SPIRIT BEAR

being shot as some kind of terrible murderous creature of the night. Which they are not by the way.

Every man and woman has deep inside of them an urge for the wild places. This gives most of them peace and a sense of inner being. Over three-million a year leave their concrete jungles and head for The Yellowstone National Park and its environs. You know why most come here? Because there are suppose to be Bears there to see.

Many of the strange people realize the mistakes of the past and they are trying to correct it. The land was dug up, the game killed, and the fish were taken out of the picture with dams in their rivers. Trying to put all this back together is very expensive, yet they must do this if we are to survive as a living creature. This planet is home and until we can find a way to travel into space many thousands of times faster than the speed of light we are stuck here. The billions that we spend playing around in space would be better spent repairing our home.

The strange people and the people's populations are out of control for the size of this planet. They still breed year round when a child is wanted only 25% of the time anyway. Most of the rest are conceived out of lust and self fulfillment. For many years the government has encouraged the over population by paying extra welfare money for each child and giving tax breaks for large families. The welfare is slowly being stopped or modified drastically. Some mothers have to leave homes to work which means putting their children in the care of others to raise them. These "others" are often non caring or wrong for the child to be around to begin with. A few are even perverts.

GRIZZLY, THE SPIRIT BEAR

Even us Grizzlies with twenty year live spans, know that a mother needs to be with their cubs for two or three years until they can fend for themselves.

The strange people have over two-million of their own people locked up in cages. These people are mostly the result of the mothers and fathers not being there to raise their children.

The human race was given the position as the caretakers of the earth and all the wildlife found therein. So far they have failed by making the same mistakes time and time again. There are limits to what the earth and the life on it can stand. In some areas we have reached the point where nothing can live because of the poisoned air, ozone depletion, fouled water, contaminated earth, and forests removed. The list is long and growing by the day. It will not be long at this rate before our lack of husbandry of our natural resources is going to jump up and slap us in the face.

Instead of having three gas hog cars and trucks in your driveway, try putting in a few trees and a bird feeder. You will find more enjoyment in these little things.

All we Grizzlies ask is that you give us a little space that hasn't faced the plow and saw. We will be there for you to come and visit. We know that you name many of your sports teams and even your cars after those of us in the wild, so some of you must still care.

We are like grapes on the vine. If the vine withers, we drop off first. We are at your mercy. So wake the up and do your jobs. Do what the Creator has asked you to do and take

GRIZZLY, THE SPIRIT BEAR

care of this earth and the creatures that depend upon your stewardship. And please do not take us Grizzly Bears off the endangered species list for now. OK?

THE GRIZZLIES

PHOTO GALLERY

The Author & *Kanga* thinking about leaving Grizzly country a couple of miles down from the South Gate of the Yellowstone National Park. The bare trees in the background are the result of the 1988 fire.

The Author at one of his favorite fishing spots on Lake Whatever. The Walleye that I have here is a wall hanger, which is huge for Wyoming.

Kanga meditating about going for a hunt. Her nose tells her about all that is around her.

GRIZZLY, THE SPIRIT BEAR

The Author at one of his special high mountain lakes.

GRIZZLY, THE SPIRIT BEAR

THE BEST EATING FISH IN THE WORLD

These Walleye are very nice ones and the finest table fare anywhere in the fishing world. Plus, they are fun to catch, sometimes I even believe that they can think. They come from what lake was it? Oh! Yea! It was in Wyoming.

GRIZZLY, THE SPIRIT BEAR

WYOMING ICE FISHING

    These fish are Yellow Perch and Crappies from Lake Guess Who? It might seem that someone was greedy and took too many fish. The limit on these fish is fifty each, with good reason. Once they are established in a lake, they need to be heavily fished due to being such prolific breeders.

GRIZZLY, THE SPIRIT BEAR

Some lakes in Wyoming are full of these fish which have become stunted in their growth. In other words, they stay small all their lives due to over population and under fishing. The food sources don't allow them to grow to the size of the ones I caught, which is on the high side of average.

Believe me, not one bite of those fish were wasted. They are the second best eating fish in the world. At least, I think so. I have fished over most of the planet and should know.

GRIZZLY, THE SPIRIT BEAR

A MIXED BAG OF FISH IN WYOMING

A stray Crappie, three "Ling," and six Walleye, all from Lake Whatever. I had out of town guests coming for a fish fry, so you guessed it, another hard day fishing. A "Ling" is a strange critter. It looks half Eel, half Catfish, and maybe even snake like. They are called Wyoming Lobster by many who catch them. The flesh is white and delicious like Lobster.

GRIZZLY, THE SPIRIT BEAR

PS Who knows, the author might just give up the location of some of his fishing spots if you buy the book. I put the fishing pictures in the book for those who love to fish and eat what they catch. (See page 84 for details.)

Deer in the snow in the Author's backyard.

The Author is helping some of his wild friends make it through the winter in Story, WY. There are more Deer in the area than there is wild food to sustain them.

GRIZZLY, THE SPIRIT BEAR

ACKNOWLEDGMENTS

LZ MERCY
HOMELESS VETERANS' PROGRAM
POST OFFICE BOX 529
MEDICINE BOW, WYOMING 82329
307-379-2339

DON'T FORGET YOUR BUDDY

"Don't Forget Your Buddy."

Rusty Moede is the President of the Board of Directors for LZ Mercy, Inc.

GRIZZLY, THE SPIRIT BEAR

This book's completion was in large part due to efforts of Rusty Moede and his staff (Marine support), and Ed Graham of Graham Consulting Services, Inc. (GCSI) for his editing and formatting. You can contact GCSI by E-Mail at gcsi@trib.com or visit their web site at http://www.medicinebow.org/GCSI/. They did the typing, editing, setups, and the many other chores associated with getting this book published and distributed.

In the military we have a saying. It is "Organize, Terrorize, and Supervise." He did all of these things and did them well.

Part of the sales from this book will go to LZ Mercy. This Veterans' Program was started by Rusty for America's Veterans. Many of these Veterans are still out there hiding in places like the Yellowstone, the streets of every American city, and their environs. There are over 400,000 Viet Nam Vets in the prisons across America. A place like LZ Mercy is a God send. That is, if and when these Vets are ever released.

LZ Mercy isn't a flop house for the homeless Vets, but designed to train Vets over the course of a year for reentry into society. "You have to want it" to get into the program.

By the way, Rusty is an Ordained Minister who conducts prison services for Veterans in the Wyoming State Pen.

Thanks Ole Army Guy,

The Griz

GRIZZLY, THE SPIRIT BEAR

Tony Del Ray
A friend who can deliver. Thank you for your support.

To a good friend who I have not known for long but she carry the word well. 4/2010 always your Frend Tony Del Ray

GRIZZLY, THE SPIRIT BEAR

A special acknowledgment to:

Charlie Craighead for his Grizzly photos which are contained inside of this book.

Perry White for his magnificent illustrations which are also contained inside of this book.

Robert O. Marshall, III for his front and back cover photos for this book. They relay the majasty of the Grizzly Bear.

GRIZZLY, THE SPIRIT BEAR

HOW TO GET EXTRA COPIES OF THIS BOOK BY MAIL:

Send a check for $12.00, plus $4.00 shipping and handling to the following:

The Griz. Fund 469-56-48
C/O LZ Mercy
Homeless Veterans' Program
P.O. Box 529
Medicine Bow, WY 82329-0529

Visit the LZ Mercy web site for more information.

http://medicinebow.org/LZMercy/index.htm

LZ Mercy is an IRS designated 501.C.3 nonprofit organization.